Cars

PUBLISHERS

CONTENTS

TEXT
ENZO RIZZO

GRAPHIC DESIGN
PAOLA PIACCO

EDITORIAL ASSISTANT
GIORGIA RAINERI

INTRODUCTION

From a carriage with a combustion engine to a vehicle to drive. This is the journey on which the automobile, with its innovative nature, has accompanied the evolution of society, humanity and its lifestyle. From 1886, the year zero, when Gottlieb Daimler's vehicle made its debut, the automobile has been the protagonist of many of the events that have marked the history of mankind. It has lived through wars, revolutions of thought, youth movements and social changes, adapting itself each time to the demands of the era: it is enough to think of its conversion into a military vehicle, which was possible because the automobile had proved itself to be reliable and robust. Speed came after: the need for mobility led to the building of automobiles able to travel long distances without any difficulties. Once mechanical strength was attained, then it became time to cover as many miles as possible in the shortest possible time.

1 The Mercedes 300 SL "Gullwing" makes its debut in New York in 1954.

2-3 The Alfa Romeo 2500 Super Sport 6C of 1939.

4
An early-twentieth century Peugeot advertisement.

4-5
The Bugatti Veyron from 2008, the road car that broke the 1,000hp barrier.

6-7
The unforgettable Laurel and Hardy in a Ford Model T from 1929.

8-9
The blue Viper from 2006 with white stripes, the pure spirit of American muscle cars.

Competitions are born to satisfy the demand for challenge, and research expands to include shape and form, which favors the aerodynamics of competition models. More and more attention is paid to aesthetics for road automobiles. Design centers are established: this is the evolution from panel beater to coachbuilder to designer. The desire for beauty is strong, especially after wars, oil crises, recessions and conflict. Reconstruction, reconversions, the Dolce Vita all stem from this. A symbol of progress and social mobility, the automobile grows up and starts to consider safety and the environment. Electronics come into play and prove to be a huge benefit, improving performance and comfort. All the way to the driverless automobile, the great challenge of the third millennium.

Chapter 1

FROM THE EARLY DAYS
TO DESIGN CENTERS

10
Karl Benz in his automobile in 1886: the model that marked year zero
in the history of four wheels.

HORSE, WAGON, COACH, AUTOMOBILE. THIS IS THE EVOLUTION OF THE MEANS OF LOCOMOTION, WHICH GAVE RISE TO THE REVOLUTION OF MAN AS AN INDIVIDUAL ABLE TO MOVE FROM ONE PLACE TO ANOTHER USING HIS OWN VEHICLE. OVER THE DECADES, AUTOMOBILES HAVE BECOME A SYMBOL OF FREEDOM, SOCIAL STATUS, PROGRESS, IDEOLOGY, COMPETITION AND VALUES ASSIGNED BY THE MEN WHO BUILT THEM FOR OTHER MEN WHO OWNED AND DROVE THEM. THE YEAR ZERO FOR AUTOMOBILES IS 1886, WHEN WHAT WE MEAN BY AUTOMOBILE BECAME A MEANS OF TRANSPORT WITH FOUR WHEELS, A STEERING WHEEL, AN INTERNAL-COMBUSTION ENGINE AND THE POSSIBILITY TO CARRY A PASSENGER SITTING COMFORTABLY IN THE DIRECTION OF TRAVEL. AT FIRST, EXPERIMENTS CAME THICK AND FAST, SUCH AS THE CUGNOT TRACTOR IN 1769, A MILITARY STEAM VEHICLE FOR TRANSPORTING ARTILLERY, OR THE BORDINO STEAM CARRIAGE IN 1854. THE FIRST EVER AUTOMOBILE, HOWEVER, IS THE ONE PATENTED BY KARL BENZ IN 1886. THE GERMAN WOULD GO ON TO BECOME ONE OF THE ARCHITECTS OF WHAT HAS NOW BECOME, AFTER MANY ADVENTURES, MERCEDES-BENZ.

12
Daimler advertisement for the first fast internal-combustion engine, suitable for boats and automobiles.

12-13
The Daimler production line: sales increased thanks to sporting successes.

The name Mercedes comes from Mercedes Jellinek, the daughter of diplomat, automobile enthusiast and salesman Emil, who with foresight and intuition grasped the potential and performance of the Daimler models, commissioning increasingly powerful automobiles, which went on to achieve substantial sporting success and equally substantial sales as a result. In the years after 1886, Daimler's ideas spread rapidly beyond the borders of Germany: in France there were Peugeot and Panhard & Levassor, in Italy Giovanni Agnelli, while in Great Britain, Daimler set up an affiliated company.

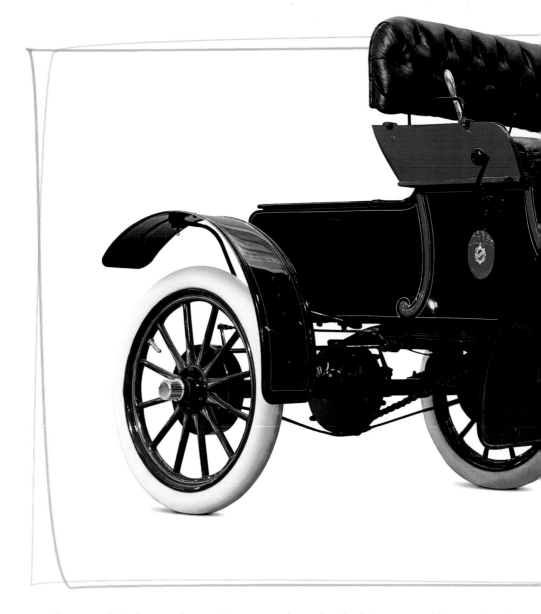

The automobile, then, was born in Germany and quickly found its way to France, Italy and Great Britain, while the United States started off a little later, at the beginning of the twentieth century, but then never looked back. At the outbreak of the First World War, when the automobile was well on the way to becoming a proper industry, there were already a million and a half automobiles circulating in the world, produced mostly by automobile manufacturers who are still the market leaders today, such as Ford, Fiat, Mercedes, Peugeot and Rolls-Royce. The character-icons who created them, though, very often come from completely different worlds: Gottlieb Daimler was a gunsmith; the founder of Fiat, Giovanni Agnelli, a cavalry officer; Karl Benz and Ransom Olds of Oldsmobile, mechanics; Christian Schmidt and Heinrich Stoll, finally, who would contribute to the birth of Audi, were industrial textile makers.

MERCEDES
GRAND PRIX
DE L'A.C.F
DIEPPE
1908
35
HENRI
08 RUDAUX
IMP. D'ART L. LAFONTAINE, PARIS.
1er LAUTENSCHLAGER
5me PÖGE
RECORD DU TOUR
SALZER 126 km 500 A L'HEURE
TOUS SUR
PNEU
MICHELIN
SOCIETE MERCEDES
39 RUE LA BOETIE · 70 AVue DES CHAMPS-ELYSEES

16
A Mercedes advertisement, celebrating the results at the Automobile Club of France
GP, which took place in 1908 in Dieppe.

17
One-line starting grid for an automobile race. It is 1903 and the circuits
are still not established.

Henry Ford was a locomo-
tive repairman. In the early
years of its life the automobile
was already using the majority
of mechanical inventions (apart
from the electronics) which
would come down to our own
time with a degree of evolu-

tion, obviously: for example, the De Dion tube for wheel axles dates back to 1881 and the
company created by the Marquis Jules-Albert De Dion and Georges Bouton, founder of
the Automobile Club de France, the first automobile association in the world to organize
automobile racing, as well as the first annual Grand Prix. 1853 instead saw the inven-
tion of the spark-ignition engine by the Italians Eugenio Barsanti and Felice Matteucci,
who deposited a record of the construction of the engine at the Georgofili Academy in
Florence, patented in Great Britain the following year. In 1882 another Italian, Enrico Zeno
Bernardi, patented the gasoline internal-combustion engine; while in 1876 the traveling
salesman Nikolaus August Otto invented the four-stroke Otto-cycle engine. And if today
there is a lot of talk about pollution and methods are being studied for the widespread
distribution of electric vehicles, it is surprising to think that in 1894 in New York City electric
taxis were already in service.

18
Longer, more comfortable automobiles with more seats for passengers: the Ford Model K from 1907.

19
Henry Ford at the start of the twentieth century, aboard one of his vehicles in front of the factory entrance.

The industrialization of the automobile began in the early 1900s and saw Henry Ford as its leading player: automobiles finally had all four wheels of the same size and could thus be definitively distinguished from coaches, which had bigger rear wheels. The Ford Model T was a primary and fundamental model in automotive history: it introduced the concept of the assembly line, that is, of the mass production of modern times, and with more than 15 million produced from 1908 to 1928, it effectively motorized the United States. Those were the years, those leading up to the First World War, which saw the spread of the Torpedo, a model that linked the baquet and touring car of the early years with the grand tourers and convertibles of the 1920s and 30s. The Torpedo is a long automobile, suitable for long trips, with a soft top to provide shelter from the elements.

The Chevrolet Classic Six of 1910 and the 1913 Lancia Theta Torpedo are the best examples of this class, which, however, soon had to adapt to the needs of war, being used for the transport of officers or the wounded and acquiring tracks, armor and enclosed chassis. The period after the First World War and the Great Depression of 1929 triggered by the collapse of the stock market on Wall Street also greatly affected the automobile: in the United States there was a desire for beauty and happiness, elements which in terms of automobiles transform into models that are comfortable and aesthetically appealing, like the Duesenberg. In Europe, instead, German manufacturers were affected more than others by the conflict, but the weaker producers in general were dealt a fatal blow in 1929. This was a year, though, in

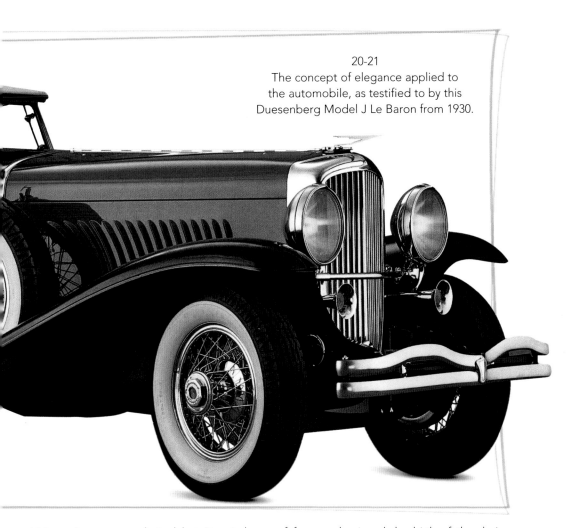

20-21
The concept of elegance applied to
the automobile, as testified to by this
Duesenberg Model J Le Baron from 1930.

which another name made its debut: Bayerische Motoren Werke (BMW), a leader in aircraft engines, which in 1928 acquired Fahrzeugfabrik Eisenach, producer of the Dixi 3/15. BMW, given the times, threw itself into producing smaller and cheaper automobiles. But it was across the ocean that the "first rebirth" of the automobile begins. The crisis of 1929 brought new ideas and a desire for change; the pursuit of beauty of form underpinned the birth of the design centers, where young designers are entrusted with giving life to automobiles that come with their own unmistakable style, in a demonstration of their shared trademark; this method is now called family feeling. The merit for having first recognized the importance of the concept of the design center can be attributed to Alfred P. Sloan, president of General Motors.

Chapter 2

THE GT ERA, BETWEEN WAR AND REBIRTH

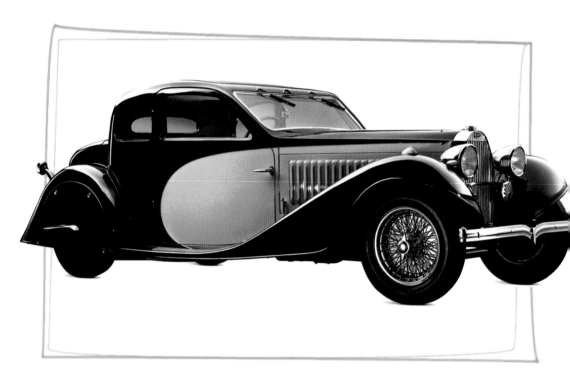

22
It replaced the Type 49 and was born from a design by Jean Bugatti, son of Ettore. This Type 57 from 1935 was produced in saloon, coupé, roadster and cabriolet models.

IN JUST A FEW DECADES THE WORLD AS A WHOLE AS WELL AS THAT OF THE AUTOMOBILE WAS TURNED UPSIDE DOWN: THE YOUNG FOUR-WHEEL VEHICLES, WHICH HAD ONLY RECENTLY TAKEN ON AN INDUSTRIAL DIMENSION, LOST MANY OF THEIR CERTAINTIES TO ACQUIRE OTHERS, THOUGH, THAT WOULD LEAD TO THEIR CENTRAL ROLE IN THE EVOLUTION OF HUMANITY AND SOCIETY, WHICH WOULD PASS IN A FEW YEARS FROM THE GREAT DEPRESSION OF 1929 THAT RECONFIGURED THE LIFESTYLE OF AMERICANS ESPECIALLY, TO THE SECOND WORLD WAR, WITH ITS SUBSEQUENT RECONSTRUCTION AND SUCCESSIVE ECONOMIC BOOM. DURING THIS PERIOD AUTOMOBILES GAINED IN DESIGN AND STOPPED BEING MAINLY OPEN VEHICLES: IF, UNTIL THE 1920S, FOR REASONS RELATED TO PRODUCTION COSTS, ALMOST NO MODELS CAME WITH A RIGID ROOF, FROM THE 1930S ONWARDS, CONVERTIBLES BECAME A NICHE MARKET. AND THAT IS NOT ALL: THE BODIES EVOLVED, THEY STARTED TO INTEGRATE WINGS, LIGHTS AND RADIATOR GRILLES. THE NUMBER OF AUTOMOBILES IN THE WORLD WAS CONSTANTLY GROWING AND THE LEADING MANUFACTURERS OF THE 1930S WERE THE SAME AS THOSE WE STILL KNOW TODAY.

In the United States, General Motors, Ford and Chrysler controlled 90% of the market; in France, Peugeot, Citroën and Renault got to about 70%; in Great Britain three-quarters of vehicles were Rolls-Royce (which had recently acquired Bentley), Austin

and Morris; in Italy 75% of the market was in the hands of Fiat; Opel was the leading brand in Germany. From a social point of view, there was a strong interest in all that is mechanical: the Futurist movement of Marinetti had already exalted speed and the automobile as the ideal messenger of freedom and independence in 1909. That same automobile twenty years later would have to defend its leading place in the collective imagination against aircraft which, following Charles Lindbergh's flight across the Atlantic in 1927 aboard the Spirit of St. Louis, launched the myth of the plane that would also impact on the shapes of automobiles in the USA, reaching its peak in the 1950s with some very striking models.

Before getting to the 1950s, the automobile recorded the important birth of the grand tourers, models resulting from a synergy between the world of racing and mass production: often two doors and four seats became two in the racing versions, boasting top performance and a certain spartan air in the interiors. Racy and fast, in their first appearance they were characterized

26
The Mercedes SS during a race: very strong in competition, the SSK version would provide even better performances.

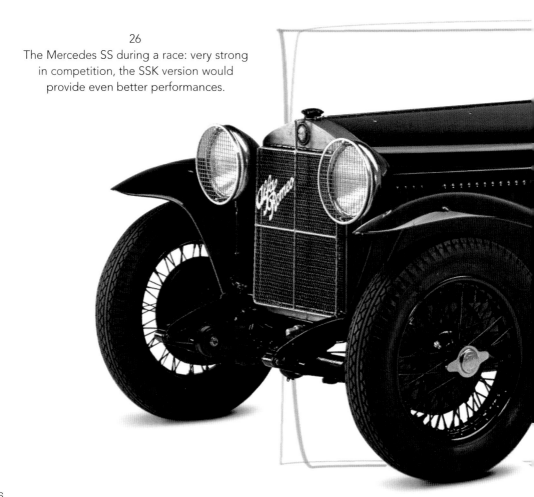

by their substantial dimensions, automobiles such as the Mercedes SSK, an excellent representative of the category, designed by Daimler Benz the head designer of which for almost all of the 1920s was Ferdinand Porsche, the future father of the Beetle and the Porsche 356. The SSK, the maximum expression of the S and SS sports series, made lightness and performance its strengths: 225hp, 7,000cc engine, 118mph (190km/h), which rose to 146mph (235km/h) in the version powered by a 300hp engine. Speaking of sports cars we cannot fail to mention another leader in the automotive market: Alfa Romeo, which with the 6C produced winning models from 1927 until after the war, models that would enable the brand to survive the crisis.

27
An Alfa Romeo 6C, a fast and successful automobile, master of competitions from the end of the 1920s.

In Germany, instead, BMW started to produce the 328 in 1936: real show-stealers in the Mille Miglia races. Both the 6C and the 328 still feature today in famous international events such as the Concorso d'Eleganza Villa d'Este on Lake Como, which in terms of exclusivity also always boasts Rolls-Royce among its various leading models, or during the re-enactments of the Mille Miglia on the road circuit that starts and finishes in Brescia passing through Rome.

28 and 29
The blue once again picking up the color of the brand and leather straps for another competition leader in the 1930s: the BMW 328.

30-31
A Rolls-Royce Phantom II from 1934, which is distinguished by the special color of the bodywork and hood.

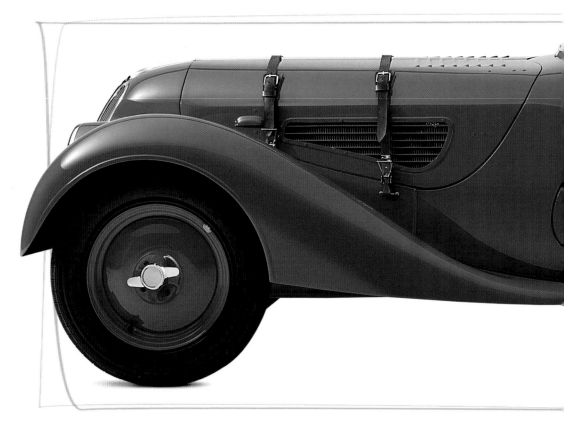

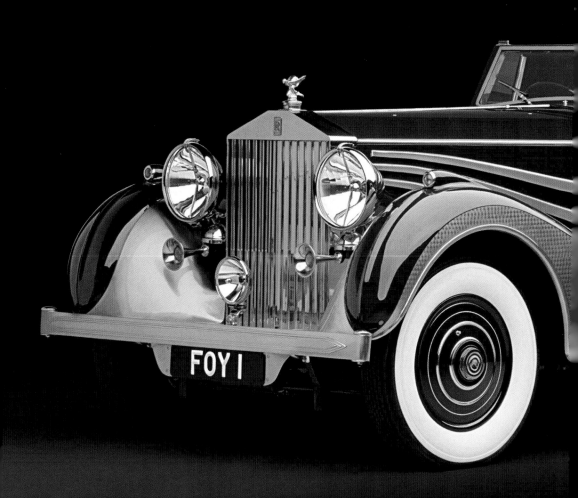

32-33
Ferdinand Porsche and Robert Ley of the
Nazi Party beside a pre-production Beetle
("Käfer" in German): it is 1937.

Other historic models born in the 1930s are still absolute protagonists: this is the case with the Volkswagen Beetle, which saw its definitive version in 1948, but in reality the project began1934 and was overseen by Ferdinand Porsche, who designed this "people's automobile" (Volkswagen in German) on the instructions of Adolf Hitler, with the aim of creating an automobile that was economic, functional and reliable. This automobile has a crescent shape like a beetle (Käfer in German) and is one of the most famous in the world of cars. During the Second World War it was transformed into an off-road vehicle, before becoming a civilian vehicle again and conquering the markets of the world with multimillion sales.

34-35 and 35
A legendary smaller automobile:
the Fiat 500 Topolino, which made
its debut in 1936.

The 1936 instead was the year of two other small-scale legends, the Fiat Topolino (or 500) and the Citroën 2CV. The small and economic Italian response to the famous Austin 7, which was built under license in many countries of the world (in France as Rosengart, Bantam in the United States, Datsun in Japan, Dixi for BMW or Hanomag for DKW in Germany), was the masterpiece of the engineer Dante Giacosa. It had new and interesting mechanical solutions such as the front suspension and transmission being combined in a single removable block, or the radiator placed behind the 569cc engine. It remained on sale for 19 years, in confirmation of the modernity of the project.

The Citroën 2CV, here in a model from 1948, intended for farmers and the roads of the French countryside.

37

The internal measurements of the Citroën Traction Avant: both its passenger space and trunk with flap are generous.

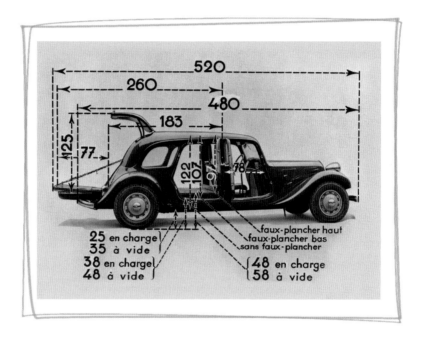

The even longer-lived 2CV was designed for farmers and rough roads: with its 375cc engine and just 9hp, it is capable of a top speed of 37mph (60km/h). It only went into production in 1948 because of the war, but continued to be produced until 1990. Before the 2CV, again in France and again from Citroën, the Traction Avant (1934-1957) also appeared, a series of models that introduced, as the name suggests, a new era of front-wheel drive. In addition, the monocoque frame resulted in a lower body in steel, racier forms and the final disappearance of the side footboards.

Across the Channel, the leading exponents of the old British style were the 1939 Morgan with 3 or 4 wheels, still on sale today in the same color scheme, and the MG TC (1945-1949), the forerunner of the British spyders of the 1960s such as the Jaguar XK from 1948 to 1954. Italy instead gained prominence thanks to three leaders in the field: the Cisitalia 202, a small grand tourer designed by Savonuzzi and designed by Giacosa in 1946, the Ferrari

166 Inter of 1949, the first road car built by
Enzo Ferrari, and finally the Ferrari 166 Touring
Barchetta, aggressive and sporty models
still capable of bewitching collectors and
enthusiasts.

38-39
Ferrari 166 Touring Barchetta from 1950:
exemplary and still current in its sporty
shape and proportions.

Chapter 3

LA DOLCE VITA
IN A SPORTS CAR

40

Opulent, exaggerated, carefree, a symbol of *American Graffiti*:
the Cadillac Eldorado of 1957.

There is a desire to remove the war from the mind in a hurry like the rubble it scattered, and the 1950s were born under the sign of this removal. In the meantime, the automotive industry was also freeing itself of the wreckage of the conflict: many companies, small and weak, closed, while others relaunched with the construction of pre-war models and brought to the assembly line projects approved earlier but blocked by the war. The Europe that was getting back on its feet demanded small, economic and functional automobiles that lead the way to dream cars, especially compact spyders. Models that already gleamed become "extra long" in the United States. But, whether glitzy or essential, separated or not by the Atlantic, they had a common mission: providing light-heartedness, positivity and fun. And, after all, thinking of the chrome and fins of a 1957 Cadillac Eldorado or a 1959 Ford Thunderbird, who would not smile happily on seeing their aesthetic and mechanical beauty drive past?

It was whole different story for the sports cars of the Old Continent, which were essential, sleek and fast; an efficiency and discrete sobriety that made them irresistible and fed the myth of the automobile. Many models born in these years would help write the history of the automobile. These are icons such as the E-Type Jaguar (1961), the Mercedes 300 SL "Gullwing" (1954), the Lancia Aurelia B24 Spider, the Ferrari 250 GTO (1962), the Alfa Romeo Giulietta Sprint and Spider (1954), the Jaguar XK (1957) and, over the ocean, the Chevrolet Corvette (1956), the magnificent Corvette Sting Ray characterized by a rear window divided into two parts (1963), the Ford Mustang and Thunderbird.

42-43
The Jaguar E-Type is born in 1961, another legend in the history of four wheels.

43
Chevrolet Corvette, the excellent US response to the sports cars of the Old Continent, was produced in 1958.

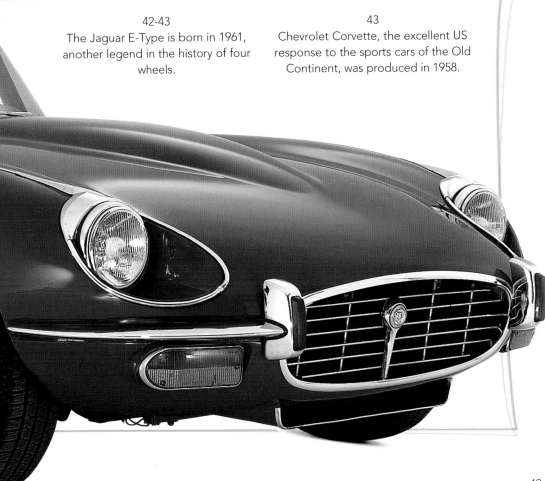

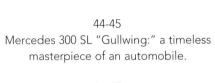

44-45
Mercedes 300 SL "Gullwing:" a timeless
masterpiece of an automobile.

46-47
The Ferrari 250 GTO: today it reigns
supreme in terms of record prices.

48-49
British style finds one of its points of
reference in the elegance of the 1957
Jaguar XK.

50-51
Alec Issigonis' 1959 Mini:
an automobile that has successfully
come down through the decades.

Other automobiles that were one of a kind and the stuff of dreams for entire generations also appeared in these years: it is enough to think of the Mini designed by British engineer Alec Issigonis (1959), the Fiat Nuova 500 (1957, the Porsche 356, both the coupe and roadster (1956), and the 911 (1963). All models that led to an attention and effervescence in the automotive field that for some of the automobiles mentioned are still going strong even today, considering that the names have remained identical while the automobiles themselves have been updated from time to time in their shapes, performance and technical characteristics.

51
A symbol of the post-war Italian economic boom, the protagonist of mass motorization: the Fiat Nuova 500.

The British began to give luster to the spyders with models that were spartan but fun (made by the major British automakers: MG, Triumph, Morgan, Lotus) or with GTs of pure elegance to the point of becoming movie icons (such as the Aston Martin DB5, which appeared on the big screen with James Bond).

From 1958, this example in the original color blue of the Porsche 356 Roadster.

Ferdinand Porsche, on the right, with his Porsche 356.

The Italian Dolce Vita of the 1960s instead conferred sports cars with the allure of elegance, beauty and style created by coach-builders and designers such as Bertone, Farina (later Pininfarina), Giugiaro, Castagna, Ghia, Zagato and Vignale. One of the symbols of this

54-55
The Alfa Romeo Duetto, also known as the "cuttlefish bone."

56-57 and 57
The Aston Martin DB5, the famous automobile of James Bond, alias Sean Connery.

golden age is the Alfa Romeo Spider Duetto, known as the "cuttlefish bone" because of the tapered shape of its rear. Lines and shapes that are still modern and up to date in the third millennium, and which also seduced the cinema. The Duetto was chosen as Dustin Hoffman's inseparable traveling companion in the 1967 movie *The Graduate*.

It was not just sports cars that were the protagonists in this period; it is sufficient to think
of a saloon such as the Citroën Ds, which in
French sounds like *déesse*, the word for god-
dess. Its unconventional and revolutionary
shape gave life to an enchanting "shark,"
a masterpiece of mechanics, equipped with
airdraulic suspension, which along with its
new design mean even today it remains
cutting-edge.

58-59 and 59
The essence of innovation: the Citroën Ds,
here in the convertible version, so cutting
edge as to still appear up to date today.

61
The icon of the compact GTI: the
Volkswagen Golf GTI from 1975 with
a 0.423 gallon (1.6 liter) 110hp engine.

Speaking of excess: the 1960s saw the entry onto the great automobile stage of the Japanese makers, with models that were finally their own. Domestic development as well as that of the road network contributed to the growth of Japanese manufacturers to the extent that they produced their first sports car, the Nissan Datsun Fairlady S211, in 1959. Then, for example, there were makers such as Honda, the first Japanese to appear in Formula One, which started to specialize in automobiles in 1962, having established itself in the market with motorcycles, or Toyota which with Yamaha built the 351 2000GT between 1966 and 1968. Then we come to the 1970s, with the conviction that the boom and development of the previous decade would continue. But there was no growth; instead there were the two world oil crises of 1973 and 1979 which drove up the price of fuel, and, as a result, the losers were the more powerful automobiles because technology became geared towards the development of less extravagant engines. To this have to be added US standards on safety and emissions, as a result of which engines of 7,000cc or 8,000cc became anachronistic. Technology sharpened the geniality of product development offices, in particular, the mechanical departments, and so they created a very successful series of sedans in high-performance sports versions. Compact, lightweight, with thrusters that are restrained in cubature and power, the sports sedan appeared as a symbol in 1975: the Volkswagen Golf GTI with a 0.42 gallon (1.6 liter) engine and 110hp. Some models underwent a number of aesthetic-sports changes as well as in the cockpit. Other examples are the Renault 5 Alpine and Turbo, the Autobianchi A112, the Alfasud Sprint, the Fiat 131 Abarth or, based on the sedan, the 124 Spider, the Alfa Romeo Alfetta GT and GTV, the Ford Capri, the Opel Manta and Ascona. Then there are coupes like the BMW 6 Series and the powerful Mercedes SEL.

Golf GTI

All that remains then are the top cars such as the Lamborghini Countach, the De Tomaso Pantera, the Porsche 911 Turbo, the Ferrari 308 and the BMW M1. A long and varied list of models that range from powers of a few tens to a few hundred horsepower supplied by 4 to 12 engine cylinders, which nevertheless all have the chromosomes of sportiness and performance in their DNA. But this period also left another imposing legacy on four wheels: in 1970, the Range Rover made its debut, the forerunner of the modern SUVs, automobiles representing a new type of vehicle that would be consecrated in the third millennium.

63
The Porsche 911 Turbo was distinguished from the aspirated versions by its showy spoiler, which from the 993 would become automatically extractable.

62-63
The Lamborghini Countach is one of the dream cars of the company from Sant'Agata Bolognese: the name, as per tradition, is an homage to a fighting bull.

Chapter 4

AN EXCITING FUTURE

64
The first European people carrier: the Renault Espace, it came with seven seats.

AFTER ITS FIRST HUNDRED YEARS, THE AUTOMOBILE APPEARED TO BE IN GREAT SHAPE AND HEADING TO THE NEW MILLENNIUM, ALWAYS CAPABLE OF IMPROVEMENT. THE EVOLUTION AND INNOVATION OF WHICH IT HAS BEEN THE BEARER HAD TRANSFORMED IT FROM A HORSELESS CARRIAGE TO A MEANS OF TRANSPORT THAT IS RELIABLE, EASY TO DRIVE, RUGGED AND INCREASINGLY SAFE. AND THE ENTRY INTO THE WORLD OF ELECTRONICS COULD ONLY FURTHER IMPROVE THESE ASPECTS. CHIPS AND BITS WORKED FIRST AS PERFORMANCE BOOSTERS FOR THE MECHANICS, ABOVE ALL ELECTRONIC INJECTION IN THE PLACE OF THE CARBURETOR, AND THEN FOR THE PROTECTION OF THE DRIVER AND PASSENGERS. ELECTRONICS BECAME VERY IMPORTANT IN ONBOARD COMFORT AS WELL. FROM THE POINT OF VIEW OF THE RANGE OF AUTOMOBILES, THE CLASSIC SALOONS WERE SWEPT ASIDE BY NEW TYPES OF VEHICLE AND A MIX OF ROLES: STATION WAGONS BECOME AS ELEGANT AND HIGH PERFORMANCE AS A SALOON. WITH THE RENAULT ESPACE IN 1984 THE PEOPLE-CARRIER WAS BORN, TALL AUTOMOBILES ABLE TO EASILY ACCOMMODATE UP TO SEVEN OR EIGHT SEATS IN THREE ROWS, EQUIPPED FOR LONG JOURNEYS.

66
The Jeep Grand Cherokee is the classic American off-road vehicle and also much appreciated in the Old Continent.

66-67
The debut for BMW with SUVs: this is the X5 produced in Spartanburg, in the United States.

This is a category that experienced a veritable boom then with the arrival of the Chrysler Voyager from the United States in 1990 and compact models in subsequent years. The evolution also began of the off-road vehicle, which became more a vehicle for asphalt than for dirt roads; they were refined with luxury fittings, the latest accessories and engines and chassis guaranteeing sports performance. Here then are the sports utility vehicles (SUV): BMW X5 (1999), Mercedes M-Class (1997), Audi Q7 (2006), Lexus RX (1997) and Jeep Grand Cherokee (1993), to mention only some of the main examples in Europe in the class (in the United States they were already very popular but they were more off-road vehicles than SUVs) thirty years after the pioneering Range Rover.

BMW took a step further and gave a sporty look to the SUV with the X6, an X5 coupe. The classic saloons also became coupes, with lowered rear ends and doors without frames for the windows, without compromising adaptability and comfort: Mercedes CLS (2004), BMW 6 Series Gran Coupé (2012), Porsche Panamera (2009) and Aston Martin Rapide

(2009). The big sports cars continued to seduce, especially in their spyder or convertible versions: the Aston Martin DBS Volante or the Ferrari California are among these.

68-69
British style at maximum power:
the Aston Martin DBS Volante.

70-71
A Ferrari California, which in 2012 became
the California 30 because of its 30 extra hp.

Exactly 50 years after its progenitor
here is the new 500, appearing in 2007
and reproducing the shape and likeability
of the original.

The automobile was incredibly prolific: many brands, especially from the US, disappeared in the crisis of the early 2000s, but other models grew exponentially: legends returned to the scene, such as the 500 (2007), the Mini (2001) and the Beetle (2011), following the success of the New Beetle in 1998. They also came with "electronic comforts" such as satellite navigation systems.

The decline in demand for automobiles in Italy and Europe (since 2011, the demand for four wheels in the United States has picked up again, while the Eastern countries become the new El Dorado), however, has not stopped the evolution of technology which, rather, has become for manufacturers a reason for renovation and launching new products to stimulate demand. Downsizing is the new goal of the automobile, accompanied by the expansion of hybrid models and the development of electric ones.

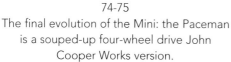

74-75
The final evolution of the Mini: the Paceman
is a souped-up four-wheel drive John
Cooper Works version.

Solutions such as LPG and CNG are successful, especially in Italy, thanks
in part to state incentives, as
an alternative to higher fuel
prices and traffic restric-
tions. With downsizing, the
displacement of engines
decreases. The evolution
of engine technology
and the development of
air compressors with 1,
2 and 3 turbos accompa-
nied by increasingly effi-
cient power systems allow
the reduction of cubature and
power, leaving performance unal-
tered and leading to much lower fuel con-
sumption and polluting emissions.

76-77
Bewitchingly "Made in Italy,"
the Maserati here in the GranTurismo
version incarnates the authentic GT spirit.

This is good for the environment, as well as for motorists' wallets. Despite the crisis, especially in Europe, the automobile shows are greeted enthusiastically, with lots of novelties on display. From the second decade of the 2000s, the NAIAS in Detroit or the Geneva International Motor Show have exhibited a number of dream models: reigning supreme is Ferrari's LaFerrari of 2013, the first hybrid from the Maranello factory with 963hp of which 800 come from the V12 engine. The dance of the powerful is joined by the Lamborghini Veneno,

another name paying tribute to a famous fighting bull, while the hybrid McLaren P1 follows in the wake of the LaFerrari with 916hp. At 600hp appears a beautiful coupe like the Rolls-Royce Wraith; the Italian Maserati GranTurismo MC Stradale has 460hp. The Stingray reaches 450hp, in memory of the famous model of the past. A small model like the Mercedes A45AMG with a 4-cylinder 2.0 turbo engine instead boasts 360hp. Another Italian compact is the Alfa Romeo 4C, an important name that returns with a sports car of less than 2,205lb (1,000kg) and 240hp.

INDEX

PHOTO CREDITS

Bettmann/Corbis: pages 6-7, 19, 57
Neill Bruce Automobile Photolibrary: pages 48-49
Car Culture/Corbis: pages 14-15, 18
Car Culture/Getty Images: pages 20-21
Corbis: pages 32-33
Fotostudio Zumbrunn: pages 22, 30-31, 34-35, 36
Peter Harholdt/Corbis: page 63
Don Heiny/Corbis: pages 52-53
Italdesign Giugiaro S.p.a.: page 61
izmocars/Izmo/Corbis: pages 68-69, 76-77
David Kimber: pages 40, 42-43, 46-47, 43, 50-51, 62-63
Ron Kimball/KimballStock: pages 1, 2-3, 5, 44-45, 56-57, 70-71
Alasdair Macleod/Mirrorpix: page 64
James Mann/Dk images: pages 54-55, 58-59, 59
Mary Evans Picture Library: pages 4, 24, 25
Science & Society Picture Library/Science Museum/Getty
    Images: page 17
www.carphoto.co.uk: pages 38-39

Courtesy of the:
Alfa Romeo Auto Press: pages 26-27
BMW Group: pages 28-29, 29, 66-67, 74-75
Chrysler media: pages 8-9
Citroën Communication: page 37
Daimler AG: pages 10, 12, 12-13, 16, 26
Daimler Chrysler Media Archives: page 66
Fiat Auto Press: pages 35, 51, 72-73
Porsche AG Press: page 53

Cover: Porsche Carrera GT.
Dr. Ing. h.c. F. Porsche Ag
Back cover: Karl Benz in his automobile in 1886.
Courtesy of Daimler AG

AUTHOR

Enzo Rizzo is a journalist, assistant editor of the magazines *Monsieur* and *Spirito di Vino* and contributor to *Il Giornale* and *Flotte&Finanza*. With his colleague Giuseppe Guzzardi, he was responsible for the multimedia work *Alfa Romeo, un secolo di corse* and he wrote the volumes *Convertibles - history and evolution of dream cars* and *A century of competition and human challenges Motor Racing* for White Star Publishers.

VMB Publishers® is a registered trademark
property of De Agostini Libri S.p.A.

© 2013 De Agostini Libri S.p.A.
Via G. da Verrazano, 15
28100 Novara, Italy
www.whitestar.it - www.deagostini.it

Translation: Contextus s.r.l., Pavia (Martin Maguire)
Editing: Contextus s.r.l., Pavia

ISBN: 978-88-540-2288-1
1 2 3 4 5 6   17 16 15 14 13

Printed in China